T0197560

THE WINNERSMAP
METHODOLOGY

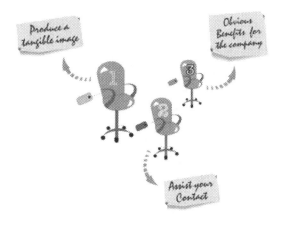

DISCOVER HOW TO TRANSFORM YOUR PRODUCT OR SERVICE
INTO SOMETHING AS TANGIBLE AS A CHAIR
AND HOW TO SELL IT BY USING THE
WINNERSMAP SELLING METHODOLOGY.

Dominic de Souza

iUniverse, Inc.
New York   Bloomington

The WinnersMap Methodology

iUniverse books may be ordered through booksellers or by contacting:

iUniverse
1663 Liberty Drive
Bloomington, IN 47403
www.iuniverse.com
1-800-Authors (1-800-288-4677)

Because of the dynamic nature of the Internet, any Web addresses or links
contained in this book may have changed since publication and may no longer be
valid. The views expressed in this work are solely those of the author and do not
necessarily reflect the views of the publisher, and the publisher hereby disclaims
any responsibility for them.

ISBN: 978-0-595-46226-1 (pbk)
ISBN: 978-0-595-70080-6 (cloth)
ISBN: 978-0-595-90527-0 (ebk)

Printed in the United States of America

iUniverse rev. date: 5/13/09

First and foremost, I would like to thank
my lovely wife, my biggest passion,
Patricia Oshiro.

I thank my son, Leonardo R. Oshiro de
Souza, born October 19, 2006;

my clients, who are my most valuable
assets and for whom I work
enthusiastically every day;

my relatives, who have given me their support and
believed in my ideas and me;

iUniverse publishing house, which trusted me and took
a chance on the quality of this book; and

all the executives who contributed content to this book,
by providing precious tips or testimonials.

Contents

Foreword by Luis Fernando Garcia

I was very impressed with Dominic's ability, through his book, to translate his own unique mental map into effective sales techniques. He knows how to monitor his selling behavior with an extremely effective model.

I have witnessed his determination and the results he achieved. As the basis for his model, Dominic provides result-oriented behavioral and entrepreneurial aspects generally associated with successful professionals, such as diligence and commitment, along with a long-term view of creating ties with clients, supervision of processes, and meeting the needs of clients.

I have spent over twenty thousand hours in training—developing teams, leaders, directors, and businesspeople to achieving results-oriented focus—and in all these years, I have never found a tool that enabled people to develop results-oriented sales behaviors as effectively as what Dominic presents here.

The reader of this book will learn to ally standards of behavior along with behavioral tools and strategic tools, such as cash flow management, client-focused projects, different approaches, management of contacts and information, and creating a sales map. These are methods that allow one to develop an entrepreneurial approach in an entrepreneurial sale.

In summary, this book is a tool that sheds light on human behavior in a results-oriented manner, specifically focusing on sales and the human aspects of sales.

Congratulations, Dominic.

Luiz Fernando Garcia
Managing director of Render Capacitação Desenvolvimento Empresarial
Specialist in behavior orientation and management focus in results

Foreword by Arnaldo Rhormens Neto

I met Dominic during a sales pitch where I was the potential buyer of his product and he was the salesperson. From the onset his approach, his persistence and dedication to the sales process caught my attention. Dominic not only believed in his product; he always clearly demonstrated that he also believed in his process and work method.

It truly is a great pleasure for me to be part of this book, having encouraged Dominic to develop his very own sales model. I was able to closely observe the evolution of the method, documentation of the processes, and the development of a unique and intelligent manner of consolidating technique and talent with the human aspect of the sales process.

It might seem contradictory, but despite all the experience I have had in the over twenty years I have worked in service delivery, I always had a great preconception in regard to sales. I always believed that the sales process was something that was unobtainable for mere mortals, that a salesperson is innately born a salesperson, and that no technique in the world could possibly change that.

This book was able to demystify and, once and for all, break down my paradigm. Dominic is able, by using clear language and didactic material, to demonstrate that selling is much more than an art: it is a combination of techniques that, associated with each one's talent, is able to transform this art into a ritual, which anyone can master.

This is not a self-help book; this project provides readers with knowledge related to the art of sales, not just a magical script, but well-based and scientific techniques that enable one to be successful in sales. And furthermore, it deals with human behavior issues—how to identify them, how to deal with them, and how to use them to your advantage during the sales process.

Debating issues such as cash flow, the client's principal

project, different types of approaches, management of contacts and information, and creating a sales map, Dominic provides us with a complete vision and order of the sales cycle of a product or service, its nuances, and above all a winning process to manage the chain of command and relationships that currently permeate companies.

Would it be right for me to state that this book is dedicated to sales to companies? No, quite honestly, no. In a world in which we are constantly selling something each second, be it an idea, a product, or even our image as a person or professional, the WinnersMap may be used as a guide to structure ideas and relationships, and consequently it surpasses merely its applicability to companies.

In short, this is a complete sales guide, one that should be read and reread, one that you should use day to day to transform your product and service into something tangible, without neglecting the fact that behind every commercial transaction there is a human being who has ideas, interests, and, above all, feelings.

Arnaldo Rhormens Neto
Managing partner, BDO Trevisan
Outsourcing Division

Preface

A failure is he who does not know what to do with his success. A winner is he who knows what to do with his failures.

—Chinese proverb

I am a salesman. My career in commercial sales began when I was eighteen years old. I ran a company that produced wooden pallets. While owning a business at that young age was quite uncommon in Brazil, my home country, I didn't have the necessary experience to maintain it for very long. Consequently, my company went bankrupt after two years; the main reason for that was that I was accepting orders that were larger than my company could handle. I remember one huge order to produce one thousand pallets per month, and the order we closed was of twenty-five thousand units per month.

But enduring my company's bankruptcy taught me much about operating in the business world. It made me a much stronger businessman, and that will be reflected in this book.

When my company closed, I worked at a newspaper that was considered a great learning ground for sales: *O Estado de S. Paulo*. That was where I learned how to make sales in which rationalization or environment did not matter so much in closing a deal; instead it was very emotional and dynamic. There was no time to think, and the convincing happened during the process. Besides those characteristics, it was a door-to-door type of sale, and to achieve success, you had to do at least ten to twenty visits per day! I mean actual face-to-face visits, not just knocking and returning later.

Experiencing the door-to-door sale is so important that if you do a little research on all of today's sales "gurus," you will notice that all of them have had that experience. The majority of great sales professionals have had this practical schooling too. This is field experience that all salespeople need to have. Even after ten years, I find myself using the skills I acquired back then.

Shortly thereafter, I worked at a company called Enterasys, an American multinational, which at the time was called Cabletron Enterasys. The company provided connectivity technology (i.e., computer networks). I worked in inside sales, and a whole new bag of tricks was required to sell large projects by phone. It was different from telemarketing. I needed to find, understand, and create a connectivity project; once that was done, we used to send the project to the man in charge of outside sales, whose job was to close the deal. I found myself using a lot of imagination and creativity, because over the phone, I needed to make the other person see the project as tangible as if he were seeing the project at his desk. Besides all of that, rapport was fundamental to keeping the project fully managed and going forward; without it, a project easily was postponed or forgotten. It was an intense follow-up process.

Subsequently I was hired by Totvs with at the time was called Microsiga to sell software that managed companies' processes as a whole. Currently this type of software is known by its acronym, ERP (Enterprise Resources Planning). It guaranteed, for example, that if the company sold a product, the finance department was notified, and at the same time, the purchasing department received notice that a replacement needed to be made. Basically, it was software that integrated all of the systems so that there were no mistakes. These sales were all done electronically, through an exchange of e-mail with the companies' information and numbers to be processed. I had to interact with those who were responsible for the companies' business and knew their workings—owners, sales managers, finance directors, and operational staff. Sometimes even their suppliers and their distributors where involved.

I learned a lot from another great aspect of this company. Today it is a leader of its market because it used, before all of its competitors, a strategy of selling through channels. They hired smaller companies to sell their products and services, and the result was fabulous. This gave me a very close relationship with the other companies, and I had to learn how to manage them and make them sell more. Now, there is a big challenge in this: these third-party suppliers are not obligated to sell the Microsiga ERP. Partnership does not mean obligation; it means that if you sell, you will have good financial advantages. So my job was to help them to sell more and be motivated to sell my product—it was a process where I sold it twice, first to the third-party supplier and then to the end user. It was a new type of game—a completely different dynamic. For example, I closed a beautiful partnership with the owner of a third-party company. He was happy and would make a great profit. But after the operations started, I discovered that his sales team was so comfortable selling the competitors' software that they did not offer my product, even though the owner specified that they needed to sell the software I represented and that there would be more commission for them if they did. In this book, you will find out how to make your sales channels sell more and how to get your product into the minds of the third-party supplier's sales team. Still, in this company, I was able to notice an important detail in the process of dealing with sales channels: these companies existed before I showed up, and their "bread and butter" wasn't my product. While the volume of sales was smaller than that of their main products, they need to be motivated to sell my product.

Another multinational that I worked for, for seven years, was Compuware. We sold high-quality products, but those products are often perceived as unnecessary. We had to generate a positive perception of our products and show our clients that our products were quite valuable in the long term and provided a close cost/benefit ratio. This was another new bag of tricks—a lot of working with numbers to show a good ROI (return on investment). But that was the easy part; the real challenge was in dealing with the common belief that the product was unnecessary. That was such a huge challenge that it made me look for answers all over. I interviewed my clients, from presidents to operational staff; I talked to my colleagues and my boss—almost everybody outside and inside the market. These common beliefs are everywhere and impact everything that we do, not only for the products I used to sell, but in all aspects of our lives. I needed to investigate to find answers. I needed to discover why people had these beliefs and how to manage them in order to get my clients to listen and understand what I was trying to do or sell.

The good news is that I found the answer! The answer lay in psychology, the science that studies human behavior. So during my stay at Compuware, I decided to do a profound study in psychology so that I could understand the principles of famous psychologists like Skinner and Pavlov in behavioral psychology, Sigmund Freud in psychoanalysis, Carl Jung in existentialism, and finally Carl Rogers and Maslow in humanistic psychology. Those principles helped me find answers for all my questions about why and how people react during a sales process, and more importantly how my behavior helped me to sell. Using this information, I was able to finish the map that you are going to learn about in this book.

As you can see, my experience in the commercial area has been an ongoing progression, one that I hope has contributed toward making this book a tool to assist you in having a new outlook on sales and, combined with some principles of psychology, may make your life easier altogether.

Today at IBM, I continue to improve and confirm that with this methodology there is no limit to what you can achieve when you dedicate yourself to your passion.

Introduction

There is a film that I like very much. In this film, there is a scene that illustrates what you will achieve by reading this book and using the concepts and principles that I used to create a methodology, WinnersMap, that will change your life.

The film I am talking about is *Patch Adams* (1998), starring Academy Award–winner Robin Williams. In this scene, Robin Williams (as Patch Adams) is in a mental institution. He is in his bed, and his roommate is sitting on his bed. Hearing a noise from his roommate, Patch Adams asks, "What is happening? Why don't you go to sleep?"

"I need to go to the bathroom," his roommate answers.

Patch asks, "It is ten steps from your bed! Why don't you go?"

Looking very scared, his roommate says, "It's because of the squirrel!"

"What squirrel?" asks Patch. "What are you talking about?"

"Don't you see? There is one right there in your bed!"

Patch Adams stops for a second and looks directly at the bed. Seeing no squirrel, instead of disagreeing, he looks at his roommate and shapes his hands like a gun. As he starts shooting the imaginary squirrels his roommate is pointing at, Patch develops a mission to kill all of the squirrels. After a while, the guns become bigger guns, and in the end, they have a bazooka that finishes the job, and his roommate is able to go to the bathroom.

What will happen to you after reading this book? You will be able to connect with any person, and very quickly. You will have tools that will help you to understand anyone, from his or her own perspective. You will see how your mind works and, as a consequence, how other people's minds work. You will master sales, marketing, and leadership with this methodology.

But beware: you will have to practice and dedicate yourself. There's no such thing as a free lunch.

About This Book

This book is the result of six years of hard work, in which I combined my sales experience with my ongoing observations and my psychology research. I made notes while engaged in research during the eighteen years that I dedicated my efforts to working in the commercial field. That is, this is not a book on strategy; it is a tactical book based on experience and observations made in the field of sales. I would not have been able to improve these concepts and principles if they had been purely based on one strategy. Tactics are fundamental for perception, assimilation, and development.

The first goal of this book is to demystify sales. There is a prevailing myth that salespeople are untrustworthy, tricky, or slick. People tend to think that good sellers are born with sales skills and don't need to be trained, that people without that innate skill can never be taught. None of this is true. There are countless methods, processes, and materials that can help anyone improve their sales skills, results, and performance. This book is an example of that. In demystifying sales, I hope to also simplify the process, offering you a guide to keep at hand.

My second goal is to introduce the WinnersMap to help you identify your tactics and develop your sales strategy. The WinnersMap includes developing your business statement, which will help you convey to your contact that your product or service is tangible—your "chair."

When we have a map, life is simpler, and the chances of making a mistake are drastically reduced. One of the ideas is to have a guide that you can print so that you can keep it at hand, and with it, you will simplify the sales process.

Today the volume of offers is bigger than the demand, and because of this, your contact has difficulty determining what has more value for him. The volume of analysis is so big that confusion is common. I want you to be able to improve your contact's perception of value, not only in relation to the product or service that you sell, but also in relation to you and the role you perform, so that when it is time to make a decision, he will be able to see that he can trust you to help him make that decision. That reality is so true that often companies need to have good relationships with suppliers, so buyers seek to build relationships with salesmen. With that, other problems can appear that you need to be aware of. When you attempt to help some contacts, it make things harder; they do not have the funds or resources to purchase, and they ask for information, starting the sales process in your company and calling you for help. During visits and calls, they believe they are helping by not telling you that they don't have the funds or resources; but quite to the contrary, this gives the salesperson hope that they will purchase. You need to be careful and always check with your clients to make certain there are real opportunities to sell to them.

I must reiterate that most of the time it is a good intention, and that out of lack of knowledge, the contact believes he is assisting you. Your excitement and the sensation that there is something growing naturally lead you to a mistake.

Nonetheless, the parties will be able to close significant deals when you and the contact are direct and objective; when your contact can say, "Yes, we have a real need for your product."

This book is a tool to help you align the relationship between performance and sales results. Using the WinnersMap process, you will be able to employ this sales strategy while also identifying your own personal style. At the end of this book, you will be able to transform your product into something tangible and meaningful for your contacts—the chair they desperately need.

Do We Have a Deal?

Thank you for purchasing this book.
It is an honor to have you as a reader.

Imagine yourself going up a staircase. While you are climbing these stairs, I will give you five concepts to embrace as beginning tasks to practice. These five tips are important for beginning the process of selling more. By experiencing these five concepts, you will learn the psychological principles that are part of the WinnersMap, and that will make the process of implementing this sales methodology easier. After introducing these concepts, I will address each principle. I will present which psychological force we are dealing with in each WinnersMap sticky note. Starting with psychoanalysis and behaviorism and passing through humanism and existentialism, we will reach the last step of the stairway and begin going down these stairs with the ability to correlate and create scenarios with the four concepts, the psychological principles, and the WinnersMap sticky notes. You will be selling like you never did before.

If you find the process a little bit difficult to digest, don't worry: that means you are on the right track. I call this correlation part of the process the cooling down of the brain. Here is the point where you will be able to understand how you behave and bring all the information to your business. You will discover how people react to your behavior—why you sold and why you

1

did not sell. At the bottom of the stairs, you will be able to see the right and wrong things you do. This is the point where you will stop doing the right things unconsciously and begin doing them consciously. You will move from unintended behaviors to intensely doing the right things in order to sell.

So my question to you is whether you are ready to go up and down these stairs. Do we have a deal?

First Concept: "Without Arms"

I begin my lectures by showing an old film. I call it "Without Arms." Usually about seventy people attend these events. This film begins with a husband mentioning how his wife is special, and only after ten seconds of film do you really notice that she doesn't have her arms. The film continuously shows her doing all kinds of things, like attending school, driving, changing diapers, and using a computer. The problem is that the video is without subtitles and it is in Japanese; the image is not so good, and neither is the sound. As the film ends, I ask the students, "Who was bothered by the fact that there were no subtitles?" Immediately people raise their hands. Sometimes people even complain during the film. I ask them, "Who was bothered by the fact that the sound wasn't any good?" And again, more hands go up. "Now," I say, "a question for the people who raised their hands. What happened to your perception of the bad sound and lack of subtitles when you noticed that she did not have arms and she could do all those things?"

Almost in the same second, they say, "It did not matter." Everybody gets the message.

My first concept is to be open while reading this book. Allow some space after each concept, principle, or sticky note is introduced, to see whether it is possible for you to do things from a different perspective. The message is simpler that you imagine, and if you just wait, you will gain a lot. Wait to absorb the message before you complain or act. Use this concept today, with the book and with the next person you talk to. See where the conversation goes if you wait.

Second Concept: See Selling as a Trading Process

In the same class I mentioned above, I call for audience participation. I get to a certain slide and ask, "Who has the courage to come up here?" I always explain that I understand how uncomfortable it may be, that the volunteer will need audience support for what is about to occur. Ninety percent of the time, I get no takers on the first offer. So I add a box of chocolate. If I still can't get a volunteer, I add my book to the pot. I always get a volunteer then.

My first question to the volunteer, who sits facing the audience, is, "Would you like to trade your box and book for this item I am showing to the audience? You can ask the audience for help." Usually the audience sees that my offers aren't fair, and they won't let the person do the trade. After the third item, I ask the volunteer to return to his or her seat, and I ask, "How did you feel during the process of trading?"

Ninety-nine percent of the time, the answers are something like, "The box and the book were already mine, so why would I exchange it for something I know nothing about? Why risk it?" I thank the volunteer and begin explaining my point. How many times do we try to convince a contact to purchase a product or service that he doesn't really understand? Often contacts claim to understand, but they're really just being polite. How do you get past this hurdle?

Start looking at sales as a trading process. Have you explained your product or service in a way that convinces your client that it's worth trading his money for it? Or are you simply holding something up behind his head and asking if he'd rather have that than his money? Would you trade your own money for the product or service as you've described it to your client? Once you learn to see this process from your contact's point of view, you will connect to your sale (or trade!) better. It seems obvious, doesn't it? But sometimes it's easy to lose sight of the obvious. Go ahead; try it with your next sale.

Third Concept: Use Your Contact's Mantra

When you are in an elevator and a stranger comes in, there are three usual reactions: saying hello, moving to the corner, and the most common, looking up at the ceiling. Today it's better than a few years ago, because sometimes we have a TV to watch. But as the elevator moves, people start to enter. It stops at all floors, and someone comes in. What is the sensation you experience? No, nobody is touching you, but it feels very tight. Don't you agree? So don't you agree that there is an energy that surrounds you? Let me use another example for who didn't agree. Have you ever shook hands with a person who stands too close, or met someone talks too close to you? Immediately you back up. So there is an energy that surrounds people, like a territorial boundary. As we

are talking about energy, do you know what "mantra" means? If you said that it is a sound, you are correct. Now, what is your mantra? What is your sound? It is one that you have heard all the time, since you were a child. It's a sound that you answer every time you hear it.

Yes, your *name!* Calling people by their names is the fastest way to gain their attention and to reduce the territorial boundary. It is a word that nobody gets tired of hearing. You will find that people treat you differently when you use their mantras. And don't worry if you forget it—just ask again. I challenge you to try this. You will be amazed by the reaction.

Fourth Concept: Request the Order at Each Encounter

When you are in a meeting with a potential buyer and you have made your presentation, told your story, described your product in detail, and shown its benefits, at the end of the presentation, you should and must ask what the next steps are. In inquiring about the next steps, you are requesting the order. At that moment, you are asking for a commitment and are getting one step closer to the order. I say "requesting the order" to be a little more formal, but what I really mean is this: Put out your hand, and ask for your contact to place the order!

But you may ask, "But when?"

The answer is that you should ask at each encounter, each time you sit down to talk.

The order is a process that occurs during each encounter with your contact. When you sit down with the contact, after having done your homework, show him how he will profit from your product or service. Ask him the following, with the aim of requesting the order:

- How is your company structured?
- How are purchases made?
- Do you have the funds or budget to purchase the product/ service?

9

- Why do you believe your company will purchase this product/service?

At each meeting, you have to show that you are open to receiving an order. And always, always show them that you are there to sell. Never let the contact assume that you are just there to help; you have to make clear that you are asking for the order, that you are a salesperson, that you are there to achieve your sales goal—the order.

You are in fact there to help him, but you have to obtain your sales results, and without placing an order, you are less able to assist him, because the company you are working for is as demanding as your contact's company in regard to how it is using its resources.

Why? Before talking to the contact, you did your background research, studied, and attended courses your company offered. You're providing your company's technical assistance to your contact, and that gives you the right to ask your contact to place the order at each encounter. It always has to be a two-way street!

At each encounter, ask what they need.

Find out how many phases exist, how the purchasing process is made, and what you need to do to get that order in your hands.

Does this seem like a cold and calculated process that distances you from your contacts? It's true that it is, but that is the nature of business relationships. Both parties, your contact and your company, are interested in making and saving money. It's important to be sure that both parties' expectations are properly defined. Then the seller/contact relationship becomes more of a win-win partnership.

Fifth Concept: Chair

This is the most important concept. If you apply this concept and nothing else, I can promise you that your results will skyrocket.

I will use this concept to explain all of the psychology principles I mention, and it will help you in the process of understanding the WinnersMap.

Before I explain it, there is another important concept behind this concept of the chair: *Synthesize your thought.*

Because we have short memories, I had to come up with a strategy to help you retain as much information as possible. So I went from the huge idea of sales and systematized it in this book. I created the WinnersMap methodology, and from that, I moved to five concepts and finally one concept: the chair. This has three subtopics that you will read about now.

When you see the word "chair," what's the first thing that happens? Most of us picture a chair. It's a tangible object. Everyone has seen chairs. Very likely, the chair you're thinking of is very different from the chair I'm thinking of. But we're both thinking of an object to sit on.

If you say the word "chair" to a contact, the benefits are likely clear to him. The contact also thinks of an object to sit on, a place to rest—something that brings him a positive result.

We have worked on assisting you with the chair, and now it is the company that we need to help. Imagine a traditional office environment, where everybody works for hours in a sitting position. What kind of obvious benefit is there for the company?

People produce much more in this environment if they are sitting instead of standing.

It is quite evident, because if anybody has to justify the purchase of the product (a chair), the benefits for the company are tangible. The owner of the company knows, quite obviously, that if they have chairs, the employees will be more productive.

In this analogy with the chair, there are three aspects to acknowledge and to implement in your product or service:

1. (TI) Produce a tangible image.
2. (AC) Assist your contact.
3. (OB) Show obvious benefits for the company.

Once you have done that, you have made it easy to understand. As a chair is something tangible, it is easy to understand why the contact is requesting it: because it assists the contact, and because the benefits to the company are quite obvious.

Your goal is to get your contact to see that your product or service—your chair—is necessary to his business. In this book, I will show you a strategy for doing just that: producing a tangible image, showing your contact how your chair will assist him, and showing how your chair will benefit his company.

Down to Work: The WinnersMap

This is the WinnersMap we are going to study in detail. If you follow this map, you will definitely be a winner!!

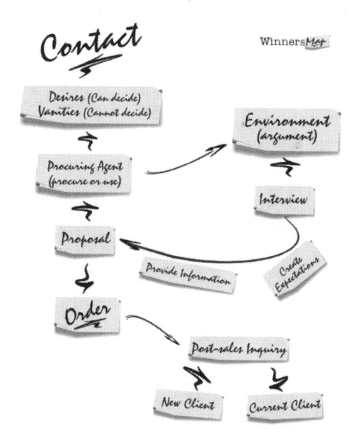

The WinnersMap is based on three pillars:

1) Eighteen years of professional commercial experience
2) The science that studies human behavior: psychology
3) The Project Managemt Institute (PMI) methodology for managing processes and projects.

We will work using the following methodology: we will examine every sticky note, step by step, and discover the psychological principles behind every one of them and show how you should apply them day by day.

These steps will happen in the following order:

- **Step One: Your Contact**—debating preconceptions; why should you question everything; what is behind your beliefs
- **Step Two: Desires and Vanity**—understanding a little bit of Freud's psychoanalysis (id, ego, and superego) to discover why you want more and more every day; defense mechanisms and why people lie
- **Step Three: Procuring Agents**—looking into stimulus and response from Skinners, Pavlov, and Watson to discover why we act and react the way we do each day
- **Step Four: Environment**—understanding the humanistic concepts of Carl Rogers as a practical way to create win/win situations with your clients
- **Step Five: Interview**—continuing with humanism but adding Maslow to Rogers to learn how to conduct the best interview and gather the highest-quality information for your proposal
- **Step Six: Expectations**—retuning to behaviorism to learn how you learn with Bandura
- **Step Seven: Information**—using the PMI concept called WBS (work breakdown structure) to organize all the information you have and apply it at the right moment

- **Step Eight: Proposal**—what to put in your proposal; looking at existentialism to understand what type of information to use, based on your contact's personality type
- **Step Nine: Order**—the closing of the selling process; the moment of glory
- **Step Ten: Post-Sale Inquiry**—how to proceed; to deliver or not?

Here are the principles behind the various steps:

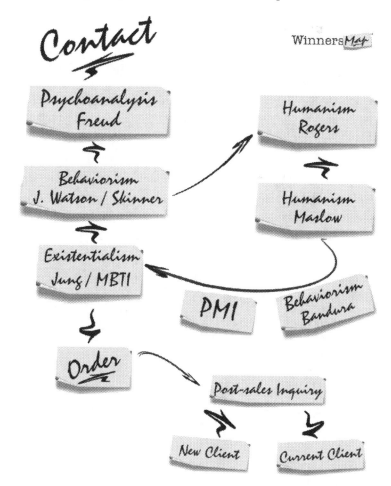

Now that I have introduced all the elements that we are going to work with, let's start going up the steps.

As mentioned, the fifth concept (chair) will be the anchor to explain how the WinnersMap works, and the main result of the WinnersMap will be that your product will be tangible for your contact and the sale will become a fact!

In case you don't yet know them by heart, these are the three points:

1) Produce a tangible image (TI).
2) Assist your contact (AC).
3) Show obvious benefits for the company (OB).

The circle is the representation of the dynamic of this transformative process—from intangible to tangible, from unconscious to conscious.

For the first point (TI), we will look at step four, Environment; in this step, you will be able create a tangible image and understand the three main concepts of Carl Rogers. These are sensitive lessening, unconditional acceptance, and congruence. For the second and third points (AC and OB), we will address step two, and you will understand why people have their needs and why people lie. Freud will be our sponsor to explain how that works. And in the circle, you will see the dynamics of step three, and behaviorism will be the focus. All of the other steps will be the details that complement the transformation of your product or service into something tangible.

Step One: Your Contact

According to Wikipedia, in February 2009, "Common sense (or, when used attributively as an adjective, commonsense, common-sense, or commonsensical), based on a strict construction of the term, consists of what people in common would agree on: that which they 'sense' (in common) as their common natural understanding. Most commonly, the phrase is used to refer to beliefs or propositions that—in their opinion—most people would consider prudent and of sound judgment, without dependence upon esoteric knowledge or study or research, but based upon what they see as knowledge held by people 'in common' Thus 'common sense' (in this view) equates to the knowledge and experience which most people have, or which the person using the term believes that they do or should have.

"Whatever definition one uses, identifying particular items of knowledge as 'common sense' becomes difficult. Philosophers may choose to avoid using the phrase when using precise language. But common sense remains a perennial topic in epistemology, and many philosophers make wide use of the concept or at least refer to it. Some related concepts include intuitions, pre-theoretic belief, ordinary language, the frame problem, foundational beliefs, good sense, endoxa, and axioms.

"Common sense ideas tend to relate to events within human experience (i.e., goodwill) and thus appear commensurate with human scale. Humans lack any commonsense intuition of, for example, the behavior of the universe at subatomic distances, or speeds approaching that of light."

What does common sense mean to you? Here's my approach to defining it. A little girl was watching her mother prepare a piece of meat to be roasted on the oven. Before she put it into the oven, she cut off both ends of the meat. The little girl noticed this and asked her mother why she did that. The mother stopped, put her hand on her chin, and said, "Actually, I don't know. I learned that from your grandmother."

The grandmother was next door, so the girl ran to her house. Before she even said hello, she asked her grandmother the same question. The answer was basically the same: "I don't really know. I learned that from your great-grandmother."

The great-grandmother was alive and lived with the grandmother. So the little girl went to her room and gently asked her the same question. "Why do you cut off the ends of the meat before you roast it?"

The great-grandmother took her time, asked for a kiss, and then started the explanation. "My great-granddaughter, at that time, a year ago, my pan was to small to fit the meat, so I had to cut it smaller."

This story represents my definition of "common sense" as something that must be questioned all the time, but more importantly, it must be *respected,* because as the example shows, it is something that is part of our personalities. It determinates our behavior, sometimes consciously, and sometimes unconsciously. The clothes you wear are determined by your instruction in common sense. If a client cannot see the benefits of what you are selling, you need to *stop,* take a breath, stop applying pressure, and try to understand his point of view. Even if it sounds absurd, *respect* it and learn from it.

As this book is about theory with practice, let's do an exercise. Write down the impression and feelings that you have when you read the following sentence: "This guy can sell a refrigerator to an Eskimo."

Is it something like one of these? "Impossible!" "This guy is good." "This guy is very clever." Or is it something like this? "This guy is not 100 percent honest. He sold something that the client did not need."

Let's do this sale together and work with your common sense. Be aware of the dance between the argumentation and the convincing process.

Let's say that you are the Eskimo and I am the salesperson. What if I told you that you will have the best-looking igloo, or that you can use the refrigerator for storage or use it to decorate your environment, making the neighbors jealous? It's not so convincing …

But as I was watching the Discovery Channel, I discovered that the Eskimos have an important habit for us sales guys to know. They always cover the inside of the igloo with the fat of the animals they hunt, so the temperature in the igloo is warmer. Of course it is not summery, but it makes the place warm enough to spoil any food if left there.

What do you feel now? But let's continue. You are a hard Eskimo to do a deal with, so you position yourself, saying, "No, I can put the food outside." But on the Discovery Channel, I learned that bears will go anywhere if they feel there is any food there.

Now compare your impressions with what you wrote.

That is common sense, and with my contact, I would not act differently. What you need to do is to move your contact from feeling the way you felt at the beginning of the exercise to the way you felt at the end. Bring him to see what you are seeing, and help him to question his common sense the same way you did yours.

And that is your first step on the WinnersMap. Remember, from this moment, to be aware and respect that common sense in your contact and in everyone you meet.

Step Two: Desires and Vanity

Now that we know that you need to use the *mantra* to start the conversation with your contact and that you need to question and *respect* his common-sense knowledge, we are going to learn what to be aware of after the process has started: desires and vanity.

- Desires
  - o What your contact desires, and he is the *only* one to make the decision.
- Vanity
  - o What your contact desires, but he *cannot* decide about it *alone*—other persons or things influence him to make his decision

For example, I am house hunting, and I have found a beautiful house. It has a great garage and barbecue area. My desire is to purchase it. But because I am married and have kids, I will not and cannot attend to my desires without having the approval of my wife and kids. My wife has to agree and probably see it, and if it does not have all the qualities that a building with kids must have, the purchase will make no sense. So the okay from my wife and the needs of my kids in this example are my vanities—something that I desire but cannot decide to acquire on my own. Another example is a contact that is also my friend. I was trying to sell to him the WinnersMap training, and it was not clear to me why he was so afraid to close the deal. So I started to ask about his desires and his vanities. According to him, he wanted and he was the decision maker, so I continue questioning, and finally the answer came.

"Dominic," he said, "I will tell you the real reason why I am so afraid. I have a hobby. I have a salt-water aquarium, in which I usually invest every month the same amount that I will pay for your training. So I don't want to regret my decision."

In this case, what was his vanity?

The answer is simple. It was the aquarium; for him it was very important that he invest his money there. I had to explain to him that with the money he would gain with the training, he would be able to invest much more in his vanity.

So again, vanity can be a person, a situation, insecurity, an unconscious need, or anything that hinders a person from accomplishing his desires by himself. And more importantly, it must be respected; like common sense, it is part of a person.

When dealing with a contact, we should look for desires and vanity all the time, which will create empathy during the sales process. The objective of identifying a subject's desires is to discover what really motivates him. And with that information, you will be able to truly assist the contact. Just like with the chair, you will see what will help him.

This concept is based on one of the fields of psychology: psychoanalysis. We will go into that now. Is important to see that behind every concept we use in the WinnersMap, there is a great psychologist

Dr. Sigmund Freud theorized that there is a starting point for everything that we want and that it grows in a way that influences our behavior directly. This energy that drives us come from an instinctive part of us, which he named the id. According to Freud, all of our desires originate from the id. And the important part for us is that those desires need to be fulfilled; if they aren't, we can go crazy, literally. People will do almost anything to achieve those desires, and the amazing part is that when we achieve one, another desire immediately takes its place.

This figure represents how this works for sales and business; it is not an academic approach. The arrow represents the energy that comes from this single point, the id, and it becomes a real desire after the person has defined what he wants. It can be a person, a thing, or a feeling. If it is possible for him to achieve or to decide by himself, he will be able to solve it; but if he needs some outside person, thing, or feeling in order to achieve it, it becomes what we call a vanity. And as I mentioned before, this is something that will keep pressuring him until the desired is fulfilled. It is such a strong urge that there are some psychological strategies that help us to deal with it. But with this strategy, I will show you why people dream and why need to create fantasies.

Freud thought that people's dreams allow them to meet their needs through mitigating everyday frustrations over not fulfilling their desires. An example is the desire to fly. We build this desire during our childhoods, and so many superheroes that we create can fly. In our dreams, we can fly, and the frustration goes away. When we talk to our contacts about their dreams, we discover what really motivates them, what they want for themselves, what they seek, and their vanities too. Likewise, we understand what motivates them and what they want in relation to their working environment.

Now that we have spoken of desires, here is a classic example of how vanity works. The goal of a contact who has worked at a company for thirty-five years is to retire from the company; this is contrary to one who has just joined the company and wants to prove himself. The desires here are clear for both, but they cannot achieve them alone; it is not only their decision. So the first man's vanity will be something like this: "I need to do everything by the book and keep it low profile so I can retire." The other man's is more like this: "I must find projects to show my work. What can I do to be recognized?" Your challenge will be to help them to achieve their desires by solving their problems. You could say to the first man, "With this solution, you will make sure that your legacy in the company is strong, and if people call you after you retire, it will be to congratulate you." To the second man, you might say, "With this solution, you will be able to go to your boss and tell him all about how you reduced costs and increased profits."

We really have to focus on listening, because it is by listening that we may find out all a person desires for himself personally; however, we must guide the conversation toward aspects related to his job at the company. I'm pointing this out because it's one thing when you ask about personal challenges at the company where one works, and it's another thing to ask about challenges in one's marriage. Individual is different from private! Be careful!

In the same way that dreams fulfill desires, fantasies fulfill one's vanity. And there you have a very tricky thing to deal with. Let me tell you a story about fantasies.

There was an employee that had problems at home. Because of these problems, this person always arrived late for work. The manager came to this person and gently mentioned that there was a time policy and asked him not to arrive late anymore. The employee apologized, but the problem at home grew, and the employee went back to coming in late every day. Again the manager pointed out to the person that arriving late was not a good thing. Another week went by, and the same scenario occurred: problems at home, coming to work late, and the manager complaining. It reached the point that the employee was so upset with the manager that he went to the human resources (HR) department and complained about the manager. The human resources department took action and spoke to the manager. They told him that there was a complaint from this employee, who said that the manager always pointed out that he was late every day and that it had become a personal issue, not a professional complaint anymore. This manager was so shocked by the situation that he decided to have a conversation with the employee and HR at the same time. The meeting was scheduled, and the manager asked for HR to bring the file that registers the time that everybody arrives every day. At the meeting, the employee had all the dates that the manager had complained and the words he had used. After hearing all of the details, the manager asked HR to show the file to the employee. And guess what? He had arrived late every single day. The employee was so shocked to see that file that tears fell from his eyes.

Fantasies are like that. They seem so real that they can make you believe anything you want to believe. Sometimes the desire to have a thing, or a problem solved, or a situation happen, is so strong that you fantasize about it. As I mentioned, "vanity" means you need another's approval to get what you desire, and sometimes this approval does not come, and you fantasize about it. In case of the employee, in his fantasy, the manager was the problem, not the unsolved problem he was having at home.

There is a technical name for this type of fantasy: defense mechanism.

Here is another example of a defense mechanism that creates fantasies. Have you ever experienced the following situation? You are waiting for a friend, and he is already very late, and you are so anxious to meet him that you start to see other people looking like him. You probably have almost waved to a person, and as the person came closer, you noticed that it wasn't the person for whom you are waiting. It's almost as if your eyes tricked you.

So the "vanities" are things that we desire but need some kind of authorization to obtain, but we have a defense mechanism that creates fantasies so we don't get hurt during the process. It was Freud that named this tool the defense mechanism, in which, consciously or unconsciously, we create fantasies to justify our actions. That explains the little lies that your contacts make. Most of the time, your contact won't tell you that the decision is not in his hands, that he is less than nothing in the organization, or that he doesn't have money to purchase your product. Even worse, his boss thinks that the idea of purchasing something from you is wrong or stupid. People don't lie just because they are bad or they want to hurt you. People lie because facing the true can be hurtful.

The strategy here is to be aware of the vanities—be aware of who or what is influencing the decision. With this knowledge, you will be able to detect whether the person is creating fantasies or not. If you make the environment safe and comfortable, the person will show you what is behind the story he is telling. Sometimes it will be a hidden or petty reason. One of my contacts had a hard time deciding, because if he purchased my product, he would have to postpone buying equipment for his aquarium. Of course, it took me a long time to discover that his vanity was the aquarium; who consciously admits to a salesman that he wants to spend his money on an aquarium instead of something else?

I will illustrate what I am saying with the following graphic:

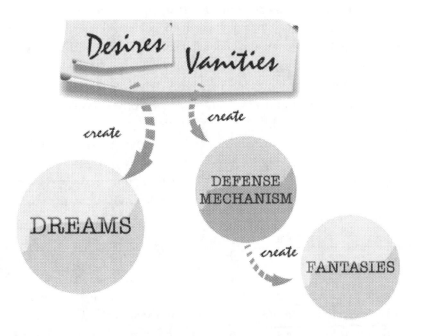

I left the best part for last. Everything is a conflict!

According to Dr Freud, humans depend on others in order to experience pleasure. That is the reason that we are social beings, so by definition every relationship is a potential conflict region. Now imagine that in order to sell or even to live, you have to manage conflict! The most important ability that you need to learn and be aware of at all times is the ability to manage conflicts. A good reminder is a classic conflict between a salesman, his boss, his contact and the boss's contact.

Here are the dynamics of the conflict. At the first visit, the salesman does his job well; he understands the contact's desires, and his speech is based on this information. The contact feels very comfortable, and he is convinced that the salesman will fulfill his desires. Now it is time to report that information to the bosses. For the salesman, it goes very well; his manager is very happy, and in all that happiness, he commits the order to the company numbers, and it is published on the pipeline. On the other side, it's another story; the salesman's contact, during his conversation with his boss, receives very bad news about investments, and the problem that would be solved with this purchase would only benefit the contact, not his company.

One week passes, and the salesman meets the contact again. The contact breaks the news to him immediately. Now is when the ability to manage conflicts needs to get to work.

The first images that come to the salesman's head are of his boss screaming at him, his commission flying away, and the presents he has already planned to buy. His blood pressure goes sky high. If this salesman is not a good conflict manager, his answer will be, "My god, what are we going to do? I committed myself by telling my boss about this opportunity. We need to have a meeting with your boss so I can explain my situation to him."

The salesman did not manage the internal conflict; he put his desires above the desires of his contact. But if he has trained to manage conflicts between his desires and the desires of his contacts, his response will be, "Okay, Contact, I understand the situation. Our challenge now is to help you to convince your boss to go along with your desires. We need to put your desires into language that will make your boss understand the importance of fulfilling your desires."

Using the same example, did you see what the vanity was?

The vanity is his boss—the boss's desires and perspective. In this sales process, the next step is to understand the boss's and the company's desires and vanities.

Remember, your contact often does not speak for the entire company. This is a perfect example of why you need to understand not just your contact's desires and vanities, but those of the company as well. It's very important to know how a company works, so that you have the necessary tools.

***

Let's take a break to understand a few points about how a business works. This will clear your vision so that you will be able to see a company's desires and make your benefits obvious.

Once you have found out the desires and vanity of your contact, it's very important to know how a company works, so that you have the necessary tools to engage in an intelligent conversation. This way, the contact will realize that you really know what you are talking about and that you know how to handle the information you have obtained.

These are the three main aspects of a business:

- **Cash flow:** This is the money entering and leaving the company; it is completely unrelated to what is going to be sold or what will be received.
- **Return on investment (ROI):** This is the amount of time it will take for a company to profit from an investment it has made. It is made up of two other important concepts: profit margin and speed.
- **Growth:** If you are able to project your entire growth, anticipating market fluctuations, your company will be prepared and grow rapidly.

Through growth, a business may improve market dominance,

performance, and marketing. If a dealership knows that it sells ten cars a month, the owner could make a deal with the manufacturer and buy sixty cars, but only ten will be delivered per month. This will change the dynamics of negotiation with the manufacturer; by buying sixty cars from the manufacturer instead of ten, the dealership will obtain lower prices and its profit margin will be higher; thus, business planning will work better.

Getting back to ROI, it is made up based on margin. This is a familiar concept and very simple. The contact who buys a product at ten units and sells it at thirteen units has a 30 percent profit margin. That is the factor that the contact adds to the product to sell it. Concerning margins, companies generally figure the lower the cost (without changing the price), the higher the profit.

Here is a practical example. If the product I'm selling causes my contact's product to cost five units and he still sells it at thirty units, his profit will be twenty-five units. Another example is when there is a lot of competition and the contact has to justify his price with benefits that your product offers. If the product I'm selling has these characteristics, it would be viable for the client to acquire the product.

Let's do the math. If your product costs ten units and you sell it for thirty units, your profit is twenty units. If my product gets your product sold for thirty-five units, you will still have a ten-unit cost and your profit will be twenty-five units. I am assuming that our product is able to cut costs at the same proportion it cost. To guarantee your order, try to associate your product with the highest number of factors possible.

Here's an example business statement: "My product cuts 5 percent of your costs and increases your production speed. Since it reduces delivery time, consumers are willing to pay more for earlier delivery, thus improving profitability."

Speed is how long it takes for money that leaves the company to return to it; the shorter it takes to complete that cycle, the better the ROI for that company.

Here is an example. You have bought 10,000 units at an

interest rate of 30 percent per year. You have to pay it in twelve months. You will have 3,000 units of interest at the end of the period. You are able to buy ten more items with that amount of money. You will sell it at 1,050 units each at a 5 percent profit. If you sell ten products in one month, you will have 10 × 1,050 units = 10,500 units.

With that money, you can repeat the purchasing and sales cycle in the following month. In one year, you will have the following:

MONTHS	JAN	FEB	MAR	APR	MAY	JUN	JUL	AUG	SEP	OCT	NOV	DEC
Sales	10,500	10,500	10,500	10,500	10,500	10,500	10,500	10,500	10,500	10,500	10,500	10,500
Profit	500	500	500	500	500	500	500	500	500	500	500	500
ROI			1,500			3,000			4,500			6,000

If you sold the entire stock every month, by the sixth month you would have already paid the interest, and at the end of the twelve-month period you would have a 3,000-unit profit.

Now, with a product that doubles the speed of your ROI, you get the following:

MONTHS	JAN	FEB	MAR	APR	MAY	JUN	JUL	AUG	SEP	OCT	NOV	DEC
Sales	10,500	10,500	10,500	10,500	10,500	10,500	10,500	10,500	10,500	10,500	10,500	10,500
Profit	500	500	500	500	500	500	500	500	500	500	500	500
ROI			3,000			6,000			9,000			12,000

If you sold all items in stock twice as fast, every month, by the third month you would have already paid the interest, and at the end of the twelve-month period you would have a 9,000-unit profit.

Would you buy my product?

Please note that the net present value (NPV) was not taken into account in any of the above examples.

How fast a new product is launched ("time to market") is also an important factor for any company's success. The faster you launch a new product, the greater are your chances of obtaining an immediate return on investment. For instance, there is a huge difference between launching a new World Cup edition soccer ball a month before the World Cup and launching it a day after the World Cup opens. Take this General Motors (GM) example. The time it takes between GM buying a steel sheet to manufacture it into a car, up to the exact moment that the dealership pays GM for the car, is called "time of return." When we change that process into money, from the time we buy the metal sheet, up to the final phase in which the dealership sells the car and pays GM, we will have the turnover of that money.

When we decrease or increase that time period, GM will have a larger or smaller profit. That is, it would be very good for GM to reduce the time it took for money to return from the dealership from five days to three days; GM would be able to "turn over" the money that came back faster.

Improved technology, a better business plan, better equipment, software, and outsourcing that reduces the time taken for money to return are all of interest to the company, thus making it easier to get approval or purchase a product or service that facilitates such a process; therefore, it is always a good idea to invest in a product or service that reduces return on investment (ROI).

Take a look at this diagram of how a company works:

Cash Flow

Speed
* product or service
* ex.: 10,000.00
* interest 30% x 12
* 5% profit
* new products
* ex.: World Cup soccer ball

ROI

Margin
* smaller cost
* justify price

Growth

Using this diagram, you will be able to explain the concept of business to your contact and at the same time measure how much he understands the business of his company. If he is a senior guy, he will give you the information that you need to justify financially your product or service. He will give you the words you need in order to make the benefits obvious to his company—the words you need in order to overcome the vanities. And if he is not a senior guy, you will help him to give you the answers that you need in order to justify your sale.

By discovering his desires, you will have *assisted* the *contact*, and by understanding his vanities, you will overcome the possible lies. And knowing how his business works, you can make the *benefits obvious to his company*.

Step Three: Procuring Agents

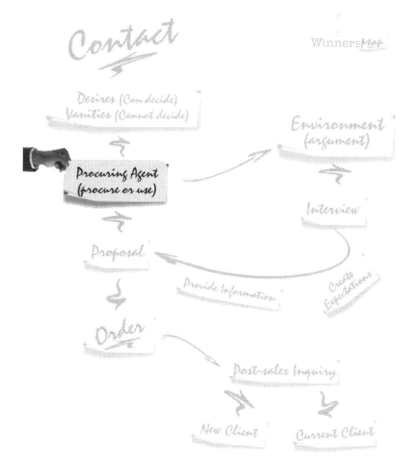

This is the part of the WinnersMap in which we will deal with the action and reaction part of the selling process. I will explain the basics of behaviorism and how to understand the way we react to every stimulus we receive. The seller should be more sensitive to stimuli than the procuring agent. The procuring agent is the person that will purchase or use your product or service. Your interaction must be stronger, and his demands will define the process. Every action that you take will result in a reaction, and the results will be seen immediately. We will focus on the dealing with this person in a "stimulus and response" manner. I base my strategy on the work of two famous psychologists, Dr. J. Watson and Dr. B.F. Skinner.

Let's do a test. Imagine that you are with a group of people and someone takes a slice of lime and starts sucking on it right there in front of you. Having read this sentence, is your mouth watering? If it is, that is completely normal. For some people, the opposite happens: their mouths get dry.

You have just experienced a stimulus–and-response action. We react to everything all the time, whether the stimulus is visual, auditory, or even invisible. We always react, voluntarily or involuntarily. This means that as we are reacting, we are sending stimuli all the time, consciously or unconsciously; even if you don't want to, you are doing it. In this cycle, I send an S and you respond with an R that will be an S for me, and I will send one back to you, and so on.

This picture shows the cycle of stimulus and response that we live in.

Imagine you are with some directors from a big company. You are wearing your best tie, and all ten directors are very well dressed too. You are expecting a salesman at the meeting. It is 10:00 a.m., and he is punctual. But there is a small detail: he is in his surfing clothes.

What stimulus has this guy just sent to you and your colleagues?

But after a moment of silence, he opens his laptop and plays a film that shows the way he and his family enjoy their weekend. It starts with a big boat, after which he is in a helicopter, and after another second, you see a big logo with his face on the side of the helicopter that matches the boat. Going back to the point, what is your reaction, and what is the reaction of the directors? Now compare the first reaction to the second one: the clouding versus the film. That is a cycle of stimuli and responses happening. Reading this story, you went from approval (his being on time) to disapproval (surfing clothes—this guy is crazy!) and back to approval (how does he manage to make so much money?). You now admire the guy, or maybe you hate him for being so rich. It's like a dance of approval and disapproval. That is a series of stimuli and responses working in you.

Still, what is new about that? What is my point?

My point here is that I want you to pay attention to what I call the "instinctive mode." In this mode, you respond immediately to the stimuli you receive; you don't think, only act. Let me give an example. If you observe a car accident, you will detect whether there is going to be a fight or not. If you look at the way the two drivers get out of their cars, you can see it. Even if one comes out peacefully, if the other one come on too strong, the stimuli will get so *big* and the responses so *fast* that the drivers will fight. And you know that never leads to a happy ending.

So every time you feel that the stimuli are coming in too fast and you are responding as fast as they arrive, *stop!* Get out of the *instinctive mode.*

Let's look at it from a business perspective. When a client is pressuring for a big discount and you react immediately by talking to everybody in your organization, asking even the president for that discount, *you* are in the instinctive mode. But if instead of reacting that way, you stop and double-check the client's commitment to close the deal if you get the discount, you will discover that most of the time it is just pressure, and the client will realize that in order to get the approval for that level of discount, he must guarantee that is a closed deal. With this attitude, even the client will think twice before pressuring you again. And in the end, if he pressures you, it will be for a real reason, to close the deal.

The real objective here is to make you aware of this mode. When you put this knowledge into practice, your contact will respect you for it. A good win-win deal is done with patience and maturity.

Most of the time, if you don't take care, your contact will be in his instinctive mode and will not fully understand what you are saying. You will never be on his priority list. When your contact is in this mode, he is not really paying attention to what you are saying; he is just nodding or asking you to continue speaking, and if you ask a detailed question, he will not know the answer.

This is a book about tactics, so I will tell you how to get your contact out of the instinctive mode. I need to you to trust me and really try this out. It may sound strange, but trust me, it will be worth your time.

The tip is to make the contact move. Yes, make him work for you. Give him your to-do list. Once he gets in motion, he will compromise himself. You will be on his priority list. With this in mind, every meeting will finish with a list of to-dos with your contact. For example, if you sell software and the contact wants to do a trial, you will do it, but he will make all the arrangements for the equipment to run your software; or he will have to give you a formal authorization or explanation for your boss for why you need to do the trial, including the business justification, with numbers.

Today, I sell training, so I always ask questions like these: "I can see the benefits of my training, but I want to hear what benefits you are seeing from my training. How will you gain from this purchase? In what way will selling more will help your business?" You will be amazed by the answers, and you will probably even learn new justifications for your business.

In this example, we began in the instinctive action/reaction mode. This mode means that you will have problems in the selling process, and the way to change that is to make your contact move. The reason that we took that path was to show that today, sales is about conducting, not convincing; you must help the procuring agent to find in your product or service the answer he needs. He will work with you, and together you and he will find the correct way to convince the company that the benefits are obvious for the company, and his desires will be fulfilled, together with your desire to make the sale.

By knowing and paying attention to this stimulus-and-response process, all desires and vanities will come forward, the contact will feel assisted, and the benefits will present themselves in a very obvious way.

Just try it, and please feel free to send me an e-mail about your experience at dominic.souza@WinnersMap.com.br.

Step Four: Environment

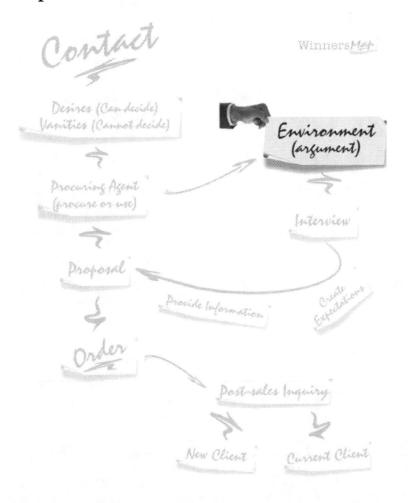

If you asked me what the most important part of this book is, I would say it is this step. Information about the environment justifies the sale; this is any information that surrounds your procuring agent. It is similar to the vanities, and it will influence the decision making in the sales process. Here you will learn to create the most important part of the "chair": a concrete image of your product for your contact. Up until now, you have learned what is behind our desires and vanities, through concepts of psychoanalysis and behaviorism; these compose the other two aspects of the "chair": to assist the contact and to make the benefits obvious. Now, to create this concrete image, we will use the concept of one of the forces of psychology that I most admire; at the same time, it is the one that is the hardest to follow. We will talk about the three humanistic positions that Carl Rogers created. As of now, few companies have adopted them, but these companies are enormous influences on the market. Companies like Google and Microsoft are humanist and are based on Carl Rogers's concepts.

This picture shows the point we are going to focus upon now:

To illustrate this process, I will tell you about a funny film that I use in my training. It very efficiently illustrates how to create an image of your product.

Here is a picture of the scene that I will describe now:

This funny film is about two garbage collectors that execute an evil plan whenever a woman comes walking down the street. The objective is to distract this woman long enough so that she will not notice the big sign in front of her, so she will hit her head against the sign.

To do this, they use a strategy with four distracting points. The first thing they do is to whistle at the woman so she will look at them. Their second act is to present her with a rose and dance a tango. Their third act is to do a funny dance so that she will laugh, and the last thing they do is mimic Leonardo DiCaprio in *Titanic*: one garbage collector holds the other so he can open his arms. The woman gets so involved in that scene that she doesn't see the sign and hits it, and the garbage collectors celebrate with a high five!

What can we learn from this funny story? Take a minute and ask some women what a rose means to them. You will receive a lot of different answers from different women, and if you ask at the wrong moment, they may say, "What did you do now?"

Notice that there are a lot of interpretations of the same object, the rose. But let us imagine that it is possible to discover what the rose means for a woman that you asked. If you give her the rose while telling her that information, she will not like it: "Hi, I am giving you this rose because I know that roses means love for you." By doing this, you have actually killed the act of giving a rose to the woman. What can we learn from this? We can learn that you may kill the essence of an act if you interpret it for the other person. It is already hard to get this type of information, and if you have it, you will spoil the act if you talk about it. When attempting to convince someone to get on board with you, there is no reason to do everything. Invite the person to participate with you, and let him or her interpret your act with you. Don't do it for the other person. Just deliver the rose, and let the woman think whatever she wants. Just give her the rose.

In other words, show your product, and invite your client to learn about it. Let him teach you the best way to use it in his environment.

Here are some examples of where you can investigate this environmental information, where you can find the rose:

- The departments that represents the company's core business
- Sales, IT, Human Resources
- The departments that has the information for our sale
- Logistics, Finance, Sales
- Where the company makes money
  In their store, at the cashier, the consumers
- Where the company guarantees its profitability
  Administrative
- Who will pay the bill?
- Principal project: the company or person's focus and where their resources are being invested
- Where the funds will be found to justify the products and services that will be purchased

- The principal project again, or even the principal pain
- Information from those who intend to sell to the same companies (Your contact may like their business statement; their line of thought got your contact interested.)
- Your competitor, you sales colleagues, and so on
- Sometimes the people around your contact
- His boss, his co-worker, his friend, or even his wife

Sometimes your rose can be the end consumer. In a supermarket, the environmental information is the final consumer, because the information we obtain when we interview a supermarket's consumers is essential to justifying our product. Once I interviewed a consumer, and I were informed that the store was very dirty and that it took a long time to be attended to. With this information, I created my business statement: "My product guarantees higher client satisfaction with automated and quick service." This information is everywhere. It is just a matter of looking for it.

Through the final consumers, we always will discover many reasons to justify a sale, even if your contact does not have a final consumer. If it is a B2B (business to business) kind of business and you interview the other company, you will find the information you need.

This is what will occur most of the time: the longer the sales process or the bigger the company, the more probable it is. Usually the department to which we introduce a product or service is the department that will use it, but you will interact with the procuring agents, and their goal is to serve another department, the same way the IT (information technology) department provides a service for all departments. Some companies call such relationships "internal client service." So we will use environmental information not to present sales arguments, but solely to obtain necessary information about how the business works and what is necessary to achieve good performance. I call this process an interview, since here we are not merely trying to convince someone to buy our product or service; in reality, we are gathering information. Of course we will have to filter information and mold potential solutions according to the features of the product we are selling. In the supermarket example, the statement was, "My product guarantees higher client satisfaction with automated and quick service." This statement I created only dealt with the issue related to the speed of service, as issues related to cleanliness couldn't be solved with my product. You cannot offer what you cannot deliver. In this case, I was selling automated services, not a cleaning service.

Now comes the hard part that I mentioned: the Carl Rogers concepts. Are you ready?

1) Unconditional acceptance
2) Congruence
3) Sensitive hearing

To capture the environmental information, you need to really accept what you are hearing from your contact, even if is the most unreasonable thing you have ever heard or it does not make any sense. Because in those words, there is logic that only your contact can see. If you understand where that comes from or how he got to that conclusion, you will find your way in.

This may sound like a difficult task, and it is. You must listen without judgment and without preconceived ideas. You must unconditionally accept your contact's information. This does not mean that you agree, simply that you accept the information.

Let me give you an example based on the film we started with.

The two garbage collectors did not question why women liked roses or the funny dances; they just did them because they knew the women would like them. They accepted and used the information.

For another example, if your employee come to you and tells you that you are the worst person he has ever met and you are the perfect example of a bad executive, you will have to accept this—not agree, but accept. By accepting it, you will see what is behind that statement, and if you investigate from this position, you will understand why your employee said that to you.

Here is another example that I use in class. If a drug addict tells you that the reason that he is on drugs today is because of an episode in which you did not give him a toy in your childhood, you will have to accept the reason, even if it is as foolish as it sounds. That is unconditional acceptance.

As I mentioned, the second condition is congruence, and that means that you need to be completely truthful. If not, your contact will notice, and all the trust will be gone. I am a person who cannot drink alcoholic drinks; I believe that I am allergic to them, and I can get drunk too quickly and too easily. The bottom line is that I don't drink. But my days are full of social events, so there is a lot of drinking. As time passed, I discovered that to talk about drinks is a good way to keep up a good conversation, so that was my plan. I took an expensive course to learn about wine. I discovered all that there is to know about wine. Guess what I do when I am in a drinking environment? I position myself and talk all night. Where is the congruence there? Good question. If a person comes to me and asks me how often I drink wine, I will definitely say that I don't drink—I would like to, but I don't. I have knowledge because I took a course, but I don't drink. Most of the time to be congruent is hard, but it is the best way. And I don't fool myself—if I said that I do drink, people that do would notice, and my credibility would be damaged.

Another quick example is people that hate smoking and are against it but accept a job at Phillip Morris. As I said, congruence is not an easy task, but is completely important!

Through the film, I illustrated how to create an image. I told you what to look for. I even mentioned the right position for that, and before I go into the sensitive hearing position, we will get more technical. There are three important technical points you need to look for to complete the concrete image. They are the Three Major P's: the principal project, the principal desire, and the principal pain. ("Pain" is the word I use in place of "problem." Don't ever tell your client that he have a problem; instead use terms like "pain," "opportunity," "investment area." and so on.)

- **The Principal Project:** the company or person's focus and where their resources are being invested
- **The Principal Pain:** the company or person's issues—but not challenges; they need to be actual problems
- **The Principal Desire:** the projects we need to run away from, as they exist to guarantee the contact's job or to waste our time; they make you feel like you're working, but no orders will be placed from this

Don't panic! We did not lose track. It is important to remember that when talking about desire, only your contact can decide what he wants; if more people need to be involved in the decision, it will never be approved, because the only beneficiary is him. Only the contact receives the benefits. This is different from vanity, in which there will be other beneficiaries and which will lead us to find the obvious benefits for the company.

Consider that your contact usually has a pain, as it is a repeating situation that will become a principal project, and if you are able to help him in dealing with that pain, you will develop an excellent sales opportunity. Please note that I said "an excellent sales opportunity"; that is, it has to be completely fulfilled and totally related to the contact's focus and where his resources are being invested; it cannot be otherwise. On some occasions, you will have to be very creative in order to connect this help that you provide with the Principal Project of the company; even if is not directly, you will have to relate to it somehow. For example, the Principal Project is a new Web site for e-commerce, and you solve something else like cabling. You will need to say something like, "This pain (the cable problem) that we solve will make sure that the focus on the development of the new Web site is not lost."

Be careful when you help your contact "stop fires"! If that pain (the fire) is not well related to where his company's resources are being invested—the Principal Project—it will fall into the Principal Desire category, where only the contact will be the beneficiary. Then, when you start to negotiate, your contact will thank you with all his heart for your help. He will say that your project is very interesting, but he will inform you that at this time, the company is involved in another project and doesn't have the budget to pay for your product or service; he will have to say it is a "no go" for you. That project that you brilliantly helped develop during the process has just been shifted to the realm of desires, and its only purpose was to guarantee the contact's job, because it was not related to the company's Principal Project. And you will find yourself back at the beginning.

Imagine someone in a room with water up to his neck. When you help your contact to solve the problem without charging him, or without associating it with the Principal Project, you help to drop the level of the water; that is, the water around his neck is now down to his knees. Now your contact is already happy, because he can stand water around his knees—after all, he used to have it up to his neck. What used to be pain is now easier to deal with, and he can work without any major difficulties, and if this problem is completely unrelated to the company's Principal Project, you have wasted all your effort.

Before providing solutions or solving the Principal Pain, you must discover where the company's focus is heading and how its resources are being applied to alleviate the pain. When you find out where the resources are being used, you will have identified the Principal Project, and you can associate it with the pain that you will relieve for your contact. The contact will be the one who will tell you what the Principal Project is. I say this so that you can bear in mind that the objective isn't to deny help; on the contrary, you should inform your contact that without this condition, it would be impossible to help him. By connecting his pain to the principal project, you can show him that he will have the same status and that his company will support the project.

Search for and be aware of the Three Major P's, and you will have know what questions to ask in order to gather the environmental information you need in order to create the necessary concrete image of your product. To close this chapter, I will use another example: I would like to mention a sales opportunity in which the contact had a significant problem (pain). When he said that the problem was in infrastructure, I did my homework and discovered that the principal project was new business management software called ERP.

I charged for the service rendered, but in the report I submitted, I pointed out a series of scenarios that could slow down the rollout of ERP. My report included the following statement, "Our product quickly solves your current problems and provides opportunities to improve ERP implementation time." We were able to eliminate the pain and become associated with the ERP implementation project—the company's principal project.

Step Five: Interview

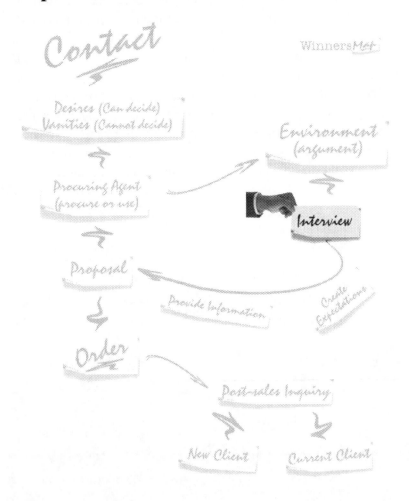

Okay, now you know that environmental information is available and it is just a matter of getting it. So I will tell you how.

The information-gathering phase for environmental information is called the interview. At this point in the WinnersMap, you should have conducted all your inquiries and should be very well informed about how your contact's company works. Once your homework is done, you will be able to ask intelligent, not obvious, questions. But remember that we do homework to listen better, not to speak better, so hold back your vanity.

This is important: There is no need to show your contact that you did your homework; he will notice that based on the well-thought-out questions you ask. By doing so, you will create a comfortable environment that will make your contact feel comfortable enough to speak about the matters that interest him. A good example is a meeting for which the contact said he only had ten minutes but ended up staying an hour with you.

Watch your vanity. The purpose of the interview isn't to show off the knowledge you acquired while researching the company. You are there more to listen and learn!

During the interview, you should probe to find out what the contact's goals are and what he does to attain them, and to discover his anxieties, why he works, what motivates him, his desires and vanity. Again? Yes, again!

From then on, it is easier to ask how the contact's company earns money.

Ray Kroc, the businessman that made McDonald's work, creating the largest fast-food chain in the world, usually begins his lectures by asking participants what his project is. After hearing in unison that McDonald's business is sandwiches, he corrects them and says that the soul of the McDonald's business is real estate. Then he explains that the contract that the McDonald's chain enters into with a franchisee is a leasing agreement where a fast-food restaurant will be built.

When you are able to find out how a company makes money,

you will know which argument should be used. As you did with procuring agent, find out the principal projects, pains, and desires of the companies you visit. The principal projects may include a new format, a new marketing campaign, improvements in telemarketing, a marketing campaign that is not working, a department that is losing many business deals, and so on. That would be like a Kumbaya moment.

Kumbaya?

In 2005, I participated in a Compuware training workshop in which the American speaker used the word "Kumbaya" to describe the moment when a group of people gather around a fire, roast marshmallows and sing songs, one of them being Kumbaya.

That really caught my attention, because if we are not careful, we will keep singing Kumbaya with our clients, and the order will never be placed. You know, that meeting with no purpose, or that client that will never buy your product but keeps calling you to make presentations—in which participants don't even know why they are there.

Nonetheless, for our meetings, during the interview phase, "singing Kumbaya" works pretty well, because it will make the contact feel comfortable, and this is part of the inquiry process. But in the end, if you have your environmental information, it was a Kumbaya well done.

I did not forget Rogers' third point: sensitive hearing. This comes in now, at the interview. Active listening is all about asking good questions based on your contact's speech. "Anything he says will be used against him," only in a good way. So, for the interview, we have to focus on two things—sensitive hearing and Kumbaya, without forgetting that the purpose is to gather environmental information through asking intelligent questions.

The story I use in class to illustrate this involves a dad and his two kids, John and Mary. These two kids here in a fight over an orange. Before the fight started to get out of hand, the father said, "If you kids don't decide how you are going to split this orange, I will eat it."

They paused for a minute, but kids are kids, and no decision was made. The father returned, and as no decision had been made, he took the matter into his own hands. Before I tell his solution, I ask their opinion. Usually their answer is, "Split it in half," so in the story, that is what the father did. But the father was curious, so he went to take a look at the kids, who went different directions with their orange pieces. And guess what happened?

John went into the kitchen and squeezed the orange juice into a glass. On the other side, Mary was zesting the orange to add to a cake she was making with her mother. So my question is this: was cutting the orange in half the best decision? The audience answers immediately—if the father had interviewed the kids, he would have known that the best decision would be to give the orange juice to John and the skin to Mary. The reason I told you this story is to illustrate the Carl Rogers concept of sensitive hearing. You will discover that by listening in a sensitive way and taking time to make your decision, you will have a completely different and better solution—just like the situation with the orange. But as we are talking about an attitude, I will tell you what helps me to really practice sensitive hearing every day.

With sensitive hearing, the garbage collectors could identify which options to use. There are a large number of possible ways to attract a woman's attention, so they chose the four we talked about, using that attitude. So what do you need in order to do a good interview? First, you should not neglect your homework; do not leave the meeting before you have at least understood what the company does; at the very least, you should access your client's Web site. That will determinate your credibility too; people will notice if you don't know anything about their company.

Now I will mention three different matters of etiquette when conducting your interview. The first one has to do with how kids who are about three or four years old ask their parents a number of questions.

For example, a father is sitting on the couch, watching TV. His son begins "Dad, why do you like to watch TV so much?"

The father answers, "Because I gain knowledge by watching TV. I am learning things."

"But how do you learn things by watching TV?" asks the boy.

"Well, you can watch the news on TV, or reports, or documentaries."

The boy asks, "But how do you learn anything by watching the news, reports, and documentaries?"

And on it goes—the kid keeps on asking his father until there is nothing more that can be said.

Using this technique, which I call "the Inquisitive Child," just like the child, we need to obtain information from the contact until there is nothing more to uncover, but we have to do so in an intelligent manner, so that our contact does not feel bothered, as this parent might.

During investigations, police must be very careful. Research carried out by American detectives (An Discovery Channel TV documentary program) confirms that in 90 percent of cases, the first suspect or the most obvious suspect is not the offender. The first conclusion is almost never correct; we need to always investigate, investigate, investigate before reaching any conclusion. Ther risk of being wrong is very high.

In the movie *Philadelphia,* in which Tom Hanks plays the role of an AIDS patient and Denzel Washington plays the role of a lawyer, the lawyer's character often says, "Tell me the story as if I were a six-year-old child," meaning keep it simple and very clear. More important, don't assume that your contact understands you. Just as if you were talking to a kid, you need to make sure that he really understood. Don't worry that you are underestimating your contact; he will ask you to go faster if it's really necessary.

When we ask a contact to describe his job in detail, we are

encouraging him to talk about himself, his activities, his desires, and his vanities.

Step Six: Create Expectations

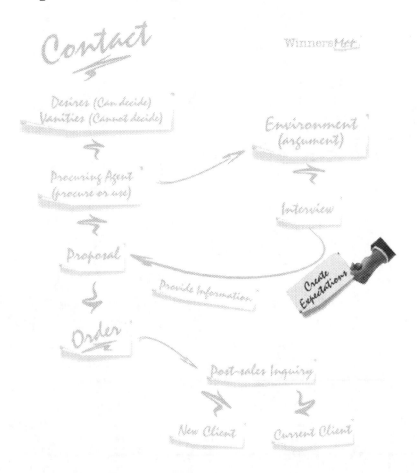

Contact

WinnersMet

Desires (Can decide)
Vanities (Cannot decide)

Environment
(argument)

Procuring Agent
(procure or use)

Interview

Proposal

Create
Expectations

Provide Information

Order

Post-sales Inquiry

New Client

Current Client

At this point, we already know how the company earns money; now we will show, in a clear and objective manner, how the company will earn more money by using the product or service that you are offering. All of the work that we have done during the interview phase will guarantee good environmental information. Besides that, it creates an expectation in the environment itself and in the individuals. People that will benefit will know that there is negotiation happening to make their lives easer. Even if they are not involved, they will pressure the company. If, for example, it is a solution for the IT department and the purchase order is in the legal department, IT will feel comfortable enough to call the legal department and pressure them to finish the process as soon as possible. Create expectations that the solutions you are selling will help your contact to earn or save money, especially by solving old or new problems that get in the way of the daily routine.

The second point is to demonstrate that your proposition will help him solve an existing problem in the company. When you are able to solve a company problem, you are creating an expectation that goes beyond the person: you are there to help solve the department's problem, which has an impact on owners, the board of directors, and CEOs. This is when you will be able to show the obvious benefit for the company.

In the publishing house case I mentioned earlier, at the end of my interviews, we began to *create expectations* by showing how the system to be implemented would resolve the issue that reporters had with the application they generally used; the slowness would end. This in turn would solve my contact's problem with phone calls at all hours. I was able to obtain important support for two reasons. First, we had been interviewing to gather information and not to sell. Second, we had been paying attention to the contact's day-to-day problems, listening to his desires and vanities.

During this interviewing process, I was able to discover important details: I was able to map out how the company worked, and thus I was able to meet their expectations well beyond that application.

That creates perceived value. When you do that, you are establishing a follow-up agent or a sponsor, as in the IT and legal departments example. If you have any problems in your sales process, you will contact that person and remind him of how excited he got with the product that you offered. You can ask things like this:

- Do you remember my company's solutions?
- Do you remember how we were going to solve your problem?
- Do you remember how you were going to make more money because my product or service was going to make your company earn more money?

From then on, your contact becomes the follow-up agent looking out for your interests and will push internally to expedite the purchase of your product or service. He will be interested in helping you to resolve problems during the purchasing process.

Therefore, creating expectations has a twofold purpose:

- Increasing perception of value
- Establishing a future follow-up agent or sponsor

You will notice that when you "hit the right spot," this agent will become your champion too. And that is a way to create a champion based on the ideas of another great thinker, Albert Bandura. This Canadian-born psychologist specializing in social cognitive theory and self-efficacy teaches us on how the human becomes an autodidact, and by using this concept, I will show you how to do it. The *instinctive mode* for the procurement agent that I mentioned in Step Three where we used Dr. Skinner's theory was the basis for Bandura's theory, and he tells of an important step in his 1997 book, *Self-Efficacy:*

Based on the S-R (stimulus-response) from

Skinner, Bandura created Se-Ri-Si-Re (external stimulus becomes an internal response, which becomes an internal stimulus, and finally an external response) and what is in it for us.

To make your champion sell your product in a natural way, you need to be in the Ri-Si circle, where the stimulus and response cycle will work without your supervision.

To make this crystal clear, imagine that you want to learn to play the piano and you hire me to be your teacher. From the first class, you love it and all the lessons I give you to practice. After a while, you start to do some extra work on your own. You even are trying songs I never mentioned or asked for in class. And in the end, you don't need me anymore; you are on your own, studying and playing all kinds of music. There is an example where the first Se (external stimulus) was correct, and as I was correct, you remain in the Ri (internal response)-Si (internal stimulus) circle. If my external stimulus was wrong, you would go directly to the Re (external response), and bye-bye music lessons.

Think about your hobbies and things that you enjoy doing. These things live in the Ri-Si circle.

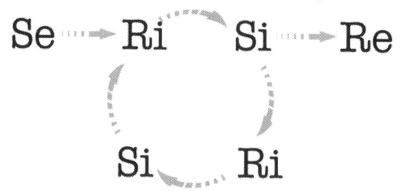

The secret is to always look for the expectations of your contact, and you will be in the Ri-Si circle. And the final result will be a perfect champion to sponsor you during the process without any supervision.

Step Seven: Provide Information

At this point, you will find yourself with a lot of information. In a natural way, things will be falling in place. You and your contacts will discover what really is important or not. The great part of following the WinnersMap is that you will not waste your time or that of your contact. For both parties, the project will be 100 percent clear. A great way to be sure that you have already gathered all the information you need and that you can go for the next step is to say to your contact, "To me it is crystal clear why you need to purchase my product, and I would like to hear from you why you and your company need my product or service." The answer will show to you whether you did a good job and whether the process is secure enough to be forecast to your company.

As we have walked through the WinnersMap and gathered a lot of information, this is when you should organize this information to submit your proposal.

How will you do that?

Start off by arranging all e-mail messages exchanged in relation to this contact, including reports sent to your company regarding the use of its product or service. The e-mail with positive references related to the sales process, or that validates the work you have done or the product or service that you represent, is also very useful. Gather the tips that users mentioned about the problems in each specific area of the company that can be resolved by using your product or service. Gather positive comments and reports from each person involved in the entire process.

Using the comments, try to quantify them with data to use as a basis for each topic that will be presented; show how your product or service will resolve problems and help the company make money.

Prepare a list of people interviewed, mentioning their positive comments, given that such comments lend a certain weight to the proposal you are submitting.

Last but not least, add reliable information obtained from the Internet.

Other sources that are not your contacts may add value to the proposal being submitted.

So you will know what to search for, I classified the type of information you need to look for:

- Market (testimonials or Internet)
- Business (testimonials or Internet)
- Technical aspects (graphs, results, testimonials, and case studies)
- Closing (information that has a positive impact)

Sometimes there will not be time or this type of information available, but practice this type of search, because when you least expect it, you will discover valuable information.

Another aspect of the WinnersMap we can use to deal with the information is to understand the types of people we deal with.

Based on the wikipedia informantion, from 20th of September 2008, according to Carl Gustav Jung, a Swiss psychiatrist, an influential thinker, and the founder of analytical psychology, there are different psychological types (archetypes) of human beings. In his studies, he defined eight different types. But it is important to mention that his studies were deeply complemented by two women named Myers and Briggs. The Myers-Briggs Type Indicator (MBTI) assessment is a psychometric questionnaire designed to measure psychological preferences in how people perceive the world and make decisions.

Types	
Extraversion	Introversion
Sensing	iNtuition
Thinking	Feeling
Judging	Perceiving

The Myers-Briggs typology model regards personality type as

similar to left- or right- handedness: individuals are either born with, or develop, certain preferred ways of thinking and acting. The MBTI sorts some of these psychological differences into four opposite pairs, or "dichotomies," with a resulting sixteen possible psychological types. None of these types is "better" or "worse"; however, Briggs and Myers theorized that individuals naturally prefer one overall combination of type differences. In the same way that writing with the left hand is hard work for a right-hander, so people tend to find using their opposite psychological preferences more difficult, even if they can become more proficient (and therefore behaviorally flexible) with practice and development.

The sixteen different types are often referred to by an abbreviation of four letters, the initial letters of each of their four type preferences (except in the case of iNtuition, which uses N to distinguish it from Introversion). For instance:

ESTJ: Extraversion, Sensing, Thinking, Judging
INFP: Introversion, iNtuition, Feeling, Perceiving

And so on for all sixteen possible type combinations.

The four pairs of preferences or dichotomies are shown in the table.

Note that the terms used for each dichotomy have specific technical meanings relating to the MBTI that differ from their everyday usage. For example, people who prefer judging over perceiving are not necessarily more "judgmental" or less "perceptive."

Nor does the MBTI instrument measure aptitude; it simply indicates for one preference over another. Someone reporting a high score for extraversion over introversion cannot be correctly described as "more" extraverted: they simply have a clear preference.

Point scores on each of the dichotomies can vary considerably from person to person, even among those with the same type.

However, Isabel Myers considered the direction of the preference (for example, E vs. I) to be more important than the degree of the preference (for example, very clear vs. slight).

The preferences for extraversion (thus spelled in Myers-Briggs jargon) and introversion are sometimes referred to as attitudes. Briggs and Myers recognized that each of the cognitive functions can operate in the external world of behavior, action, people, and things (extraverted attitude) or the internal world of ideas and reflection (introverted attitude). The Myers-Briggs Type Indicator sorts for an overall preference for one or the other of these.

The terms "extravert" and "introvert" are used in a special sense when discussing the Myers-Briggs Type Indicator. People who prefer extraversion draw energy from action: they tend to act, then reflect, then act further. If they are inactive, their level of energy and motivation tends to decline. Conversely, those who prefer introversion become less energized as they act: they prefer to reflect, then act, then reflect again. People who prefer introversion need time out to reflect in order to rebuild energy.

The extravert's flow is directed outward toward people and objects, and the introvert's is directed inward toward concepts and ideas. There are several contrasting characteristics between extraverts and introverts: extraverts are action-oriented and desire breadth, while introverts are thought-oriented and seek depth. Extraverts often prefer more frequent interaction, while introverts prefer more substantial interaction.

Jung identified two pairs of psychological functions:

The two perceiving functions, sensing and intuition
The two judging functions, thinking and feeling

According to the Myers-Briggs typology model, each person uses one of these four functions more dominantly and proficiently than the other three; however, all four functions are used at different times depending on the circumstances.

Sensing and intuition are the information-gathering (perceiving) functions. They describe how new information is understood and interpreted. Individuals who prefer sensing are more likely to trust information that is in the present, tangible and concrete: that is, information that can be understood by the five senses. They tend to distrust hunches that seem to come out of nowhere. They prefer to look for details and facts. For them, the meaning is in the data. On the other hand, those who prefer intuition tend to trust information that is more abstract or theoretical, that can be associated with other information (either remembered or discovered by seeking a wider context or pattern). They may be more interested in future possibilities. They tend to trust those flashes of insight that seem to bubble up from the unconscious mind. The meaning is in how the data relates to the pattern or theory.

Thinking and feeling are the decision-making (judging) functions. The thinking and feeling functions are both used to make rational decisions, based on the data received from the information-gathering functions (sensing or intuition). Those who prefer thinking tend to decide things from a more detached standpoint, measuring the decision by what seems reasonable, logical, causal, and consistent and matching a given set of rules. Those who prefer feeling tend to come to decisions by associating or empathizing with the situation, looking at it "from the inside," and weighing the situation to achieve, on balance, the greatest harmony, consensus, and fit, considering the needs of the people involved.

As noted already, people who prefer thinking do not necessarily, in the everyday sense, "think better" than their feeling counterparts; the opposite preference is considered an equally rational way of coming to decisions (and, in any case, the MBTI assessment is a measure of preference, not ability). Similarly, those who prefer feeling do not necessarily have "better" emotional reactions than their thinking counterparts.

These concepts means that there are different ways to present information and that people may see things from a perspective different from yours. So with that in mind, you can deal with any information that you receive. I will illustrate this with the following examples.

When you are talking to an extravert (E), you must let him talk too. Seek his opinion and use a lot of movement. He is a people person; he wants to interact and discuss things with you. He has very broad vision. On the other hand, if is an introvert (I), be very discreet in your movements and elaborate on your thoughts; discuss the matters in detail and reflect. If you notice that your contact has a preference for sensing (S), you can be very direct and logical. Talk about practical details, give the specifics of delivery, and be very direct in your comments. The future belongs to the intuitive (N) person. This person will be looking for your innovative aspects and your capability to adapt to situations; "flexibility" and "holistic" are his motivational words. Thinking (T) and feeling (F) people are very different, like water and fire. The thinking person is very straightforward and direct, and "justice" is his word; 1 + 1 is really 2. But for the feeling person, you can be sure that 1 + 1 can be 3 or 4, maybe 100. This person is all about feelings and taking care of people; he is very oriented to human characteristics, and he will be very interested in how you are going to improve people's lives.

The key to all of this is to discover your archetype, and from that viewpoint, you will easily notice what other people's archetypes are. If you are an extravert (E), you act toward others the way you would like people to act toward you, and if the person you are dealing with is different from you, do the things that an introvert (I) likes. It will be one of two options.

Step Seven is all about how you collect, organize, and learn with the information that you will insert in you proposal or proposition.

Step Eight: Proposal

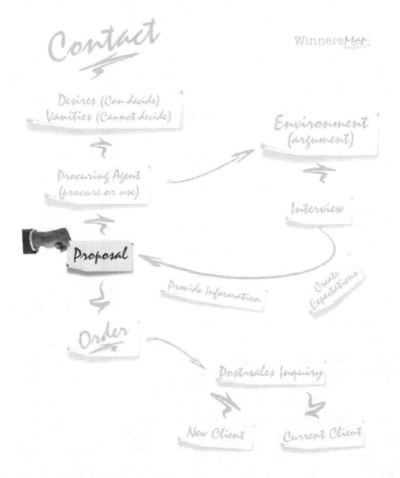

Think of the proposal as an internal salesperson, a sales document that can translate what you a proposing regardless who the reader is.

You need to determine the right time to submit your proposal. Don't be in a hurry. Several things need to have occurred before you present it.

First, be sure that you have established an effective commitment from your contact. This means that he is aware that this is a purchasing process, not a fun time to learn. Your time and his should be dedicated to focusing on finding a solution to problems and the purchase of that solution.

Next, you must have established a direct link with the company's principal project. Be sure that you are providing a product that alleviates a real need that directly affects the company's ultimate goal.

Third, prepare the proposal along with your contact; that is, put his words and conclusion on the proposal. Make sure about the exact words; have him help you define the return on investments or the benefits that you came up with together. His name, personality, feelings, and opinions must be on the proposal.

Fourth, map the sales process in detail. Follow the purchase order, and know where your proposal will go. Will it be the legal department, finance, purchasing, or the technical team? This is important, as these people need to see words or images that they can recognize and that will appeal to them. If is going to pass through the legal department, make sure you mention on the proposal that that department's approval is important to the process. Acknowledge everybody—and for that you will need to know the sales process.

Fifth, create a clear and interesting business statement. Start with a clear message about the benefits to the person and the company. Make it a very small phrase, so that the first thing people will read is that message. "Our project is to save 10 percent in cost and increase revenue 20 percent through implementation of the WinnersMap sales methodology."

Sixth, gather data that effectively supports your product. If your company did a trial, gather information that is important to put on the proposal; for example, include the name of an important person or application.

Take all of the information involved in the process and insert it into the proposal. Effectively, this is quite different from coherent arguments, which are contaminated with beliefs and training. The information you are collecting here is of real needs from the contact's perspective. Most of the time, the product or service we sell makes sense, provides an excellent return, has impressive benefits, and provides sensational opportunities. Is this all true? Of course it is, or else the company would not exist. But that is the point: the contact does not see it in the same light and has other proposals in hand. Thus, if your proposal is not clear and objective for your client, he will not buy your product.

Some more aspects should still be covered, but by taking care of the above-mentioned items, the probability that you will succeed is well above 90 percent. Let's avoid perfection being "the enemy of the good."

If the proposal is submitted prior to this point in negotiations, it will be destined to end up in the "trash file"—that is, the trash. With assumptions and missing information, the proposal becomes weak and does not help your contact to move the process forward. There is always a boss to convince or a person that will have to approve the quote or process in order to proceed. Or if your proposal stops in a department and somebody does not like the idea, that unadvised person will stop everything and call more competitors for the deal.

Another common thing is that there is always a big rush. There is not time to do much gathering, so your objective will be to gain time. If you have not obtained the commitment to justify submitting a proposal, and the contact asks you for one, ask him why he wants one. Ask if he is prepared to receive a proposal. I often explain the entire sales process, to make it clear that the proposal is very complex, that it involves other departments of the company, and that it only makes sense when there is commitment. Tell him about the various phases, using the WinnersMap, the points we have raised, and all possible details of your sales process.

Do not be embarrassed to say that your proposal costs money, because it is true. You are spending your time and your team's time to prepare it. You and your team cost money—not to mention the opportunity cost; that is, other potential companies that you may not be servicing.

When you show the contact the wealth of details, he will respect your work, and more importantly, he will realize how much work you put in to attend to him. Most of the times, after that chat, you will get more commitment from your contact.

Another important aspect that truly makes this methodology a winning one is the business statement. The business statement should give your contact the ideal argument for the purchase— once you are making it evident what he is gaining from it, given that we are meeting his interests.

For instance, it might be something like this: "My product or service will bring you a 10 percent profit and will reduce your company's costs by 20 percent." Or it could say, "My product or Service will contribute toward a sales increase of 10 percent."

It's also important to use the company's jargon. Your proposal will contain employee testimonials, comments, and the jargon used within the company, so that it can be read by any contact within the company, from the secretary to the CEO. It is essential that all who read the proposal perceive the opinion and effective participation of their group; the proposal should reflect the group's values. They should perceive that the proposal didn't come from the salesperson's imagination but actually contains the company's and employees' point of view. Use company jargon throughout the proposal. Your proposal should convey your contact's participation and that of other employees; that is, if they sell cattle, discuss how many steer he is taking about in this deal.

At this point, your contact should understand the value of your "chair" to his company. If he asks for a discount, it's because he still doesn't understand what you're selling him.

If you are buying a product or service that will help you drastically increase income, you do not ask for a discount. In other words, if you perceive the added value from the benefits you will receive, discounts are not an issue. When I am purchasing a vehicle that will be used for school transportation and I am likely to earn ten thousand dollars a month, there is no need to ask for a discount on a car that costs ten thousand dollars. The difference between benefits and price is very big from the contact's point of view. Also take into consideration that the purchasing department is assessed based on the discount it is able to get on the initial proposals submitted, so you should include a margin so that the purchasing department may meet their goal, but all the work carried out justifies no need for a discount. In short, the proposal should only be submitted when the contact is committed, it uses the contact's jargon, and the company perceives the value.

Step Nine: Order

Contact, I brought you some information we exchanged ideas. Now I would like you to place an order. Do you plan to buy? Do you have the budget to buy? What is your purchasing process? Who approves purchases in your company? Can we schedule our next meeting for next Monday? These are the questions for this step. You have done your part; now it is time for the customer to do his. Everyone in the company should know that you are involved in a purchasing process; everybody should be involved. Nowadays, purchasing processes are very complex. If anyone is against the process, they will soon speak up, and thus you can deal with it at the onset, thereby avoiding unpleasant surprises in the future, such as someone saying they weren't informed about the process. In this case, you should have proof that everyone was informed; if you don't, all of your effort will go down the drain.

Another point is to make it clear that you are the salesperson, that you are there to help to supply and share information, but your own company expects you to perform; you are there to sell and request the order. Others have to realize that this is how you are evaluated, that you are there to request an order.

So what I am saying here is that you should ask for the order all the time. One way to do that is by asking what the next steps are.

"But, all you think about is sales!"

"Yes, that's all I think about, okay?"

Don't be embarrassed! Remember that all contacts are evaluated on their performance. In one way or another; we are assessed based on our orders. That is the name of the game.

In this step, your selling process is concluded. The answer may be either yes or no, but it is concluded.

Step Ten: Post-Sale Inquiry

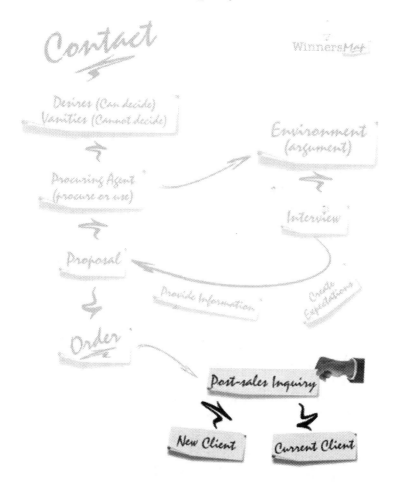

Usually, the term "post-sale" is used to indicate follow-up with the contact after the sale, so that he can become familiar with how to use the product or service. In this book, I have used this term to make it clear that you need to ask your contact, to whom you have just sold, if there is any potential for new sales, or if is better to go on to a new contact. You have to define whether you will seek a new contact or attempt to close other business within the same company.

Currently, one the biggest sales secrets is how to identify opportunities as fast as possible. And how do you do that? You do it by asking. At first, even when consciously following the WinnersMap, you find out that you are unable to locate a winner, that you still need more information to complete the WinnersMap process, or that your proposal is not justifiable. Probe further, and decide if you want to continue to approach that business, regardless of its risk, or if you should try other clients instead.

What I mean is, don't fall in love with the opportunity; fall in love with the sales process. Giving up a sale doesn't represent a defeat, because the sooner you are able to identify that there is no business to be made, the sooner you will be able to pursue another opportunity.

You can inform your contact that there is no business opportunity, wrap up the meeting with a good old Kumbaya, and just walk away.

Another important detail is that throughout the entire sales process, there should be a winner. If it doesn't exist, move on to the next opportunity. A winner is not necessarily a decision maker, but it is a contact that will assist you, explain the company's organizational chart to you, and guide you to the right person to close the sale. Finally, if it is a long-term relationship that has potential for new orders, continue the post-sales inquiry; if it is a short-term transaction, pursue a new client.

Make a decision before it is too late.

Remember that you can only consider a company to be a

client or business partner after the third order. Before that, your risks are still high, and the company has to become a frequent client.

Last Tips

You should notice that as a professional working in the commercial area, you have a number of collaborators who may help you have a more accurate vision. These include your contacts, co-workers, friends, and significant other. There is no better way to learn than to listen to those who will be honest with you. Take into consideration your friends' opinions; precisely because they are your friends, they will be sincere, and more often than not, they will tell you things that you need to hear but that no one else has the courage to say. They will give you advice that, if heeded, will allow you to improve your performance. Listen carefully to your spouse's advice and comments; no one knows you better than he or she does. You may find a lot of encouragement from your spouse, given that they tend to support us, have patience, and give us loving care that helps us focus.

Your professional counterparts, especially those co-workers who are in the limelight because of their sales, also have a lot to teach. Observe them, listen to them, and question them—exchange ideas. Not all of your contacts will be salespeople. Do not limit yourself to sales champions; observe the strategies of beginners, as they have an outsider's view that is untainted and that may be useful to those who are willing to watch and listen. They think out of the box. In other words, they have a different view from others who are living that reality; therefore, their vision is closer to that of a contact who does not know your product or service.

Additionally, stop dreaming about the "big catch." Better yet, always think about it, but don't neglect the small orders, because they are your "bread and butter," giving you meaning and motivating you on a daily basis. Quite often, it is easier to break down a large order into various small orders, so that, as my co-worker from Rio often puts it, you can "get it through the door." Your contact's company may not always be sufficiently mature to use the products or services purchased in a large order—they are unable to use everything included in the package you sell, and that is when you should stop thinking about receiving high commissions and think about serving your contact. For example, if you know that the project is long and complex, do it in phases; don't try to sell all of it at once. Explain to the client that there are points that can be addressed in the future, and focus on what can be delivered in a short time. "Focus on the moon, but don't forget to enjoy the journey." I have specified some important aspects to incorporate in your day-to-day life before we go into the WinnersMap. You can use these tips right away:

- Arming and disarming
- The elevator pitch
- Discovering why the contact is going to purchase, and why at that specific time
- Never saying something that is not true
- Never assuming (ask your contact)
- Communicating with all parties
- Sharing your feelings
- Letting your contact display his vanities

Arming and Disarming

During a negotiation, you have to set your contact at ease before you try to convince him of anything. It is like an unconscious dance: you need to disarm him first in order to sell.

In your first try, the contact will be "armed"; that will be his first reaction. Let him. With open questions and synergy, you will disarm him again and start the sale. Probably in response to some word you say or point you make, he will "rearm," and you must go for the open questions or make him talk about himself and disarm him once again to continue the sales process. It is a dance of stimulus and response, and it will be conscious or unconscious. Let me demonstrate:

"Hi, Mr. Client. Before you say anything, I would like to show you that I have the solution for your problems. It will take no more than one second."

In this case, I have instantly "armed" my contact. If he is a very educated person, he will pretend he is listening.

Now have a look at this opening:

"Hi, Mr. Client. What is the objective of our meeting? What did you understand about my company? How can I help you?"

In this case, the fact that he will start the conversation will disarm him toward me.

It is simple; there is no contact that is not "armed." It is part of human nature: when one is labeled as a salesperson, the contact automatically will "arm" him or herself. There is no logical explanation; we are built that way. According to Pavlov, this is a stimulus and response that is stronger that us, and according to Freud, it is an unconscious act most of the time. It's just something that will occur frequently. So make sure your contact is "disarmed" before you begin your sale. Try to make this dance a pleasing dance.

The Elevator Pitch

We are talking about an intake of 20 percent. In an hour-long presentation, we will retain solely twelve minutes' worth of information (if we refer to the material during the same day). After one week has passed, the amount retained is only 2 percent; that is, only 1.2 minutes. When you are working with your contact, you have to make up a business statement that highlights the value of your product or service in relation to your contact's needs, so that he may perceive its value more quickly. Americans have dubbed this the "elevator pitch"; it's a technique for describing your product within thirty seconds during an elevator ride. With our map, we learn to do this with our business statement. Initially this statement is more useful for the salesperson than the contact. Only later will it assist the contact. It will happen in this order because the contact eventually will use your statement when he is questioned about the purchasing process. Your word will be his when he is talking to his boss.

Here are some statements:

- My product or service will help you increase sales by 20 percent, because you will sell more cotton.
- With my product or service, not only will you cut back costs by 10 percent, but also your clients will want to buy more of your tomato sauce.

Do you see how these statements give the contact everything he needs to know in order to move ahead with making an order?

When your statement is not solid, people will say things like the following:

- Your product or service is great, but what is in it for me?
- How will it help me increase my product's sales?

The contact has to be able to make the link between what he sells and what he is going to gain, in one statement.

Your statement will be the only information that the contact will remember in order to justify, to anyone at any time, your product or service. If you are unable to link your product or service with the benefit for your contact through a business statement, you will be unable to make him perceive the value of your product or service; most importantly, you will have no basis on which to continue with the sales process. Another interesting aspect is that by memorizing your statement, your contact will most likely remember other details and will be more encouraged to tell other people about it (as if it were a piece of gossip).

Try it out. Write it out or try to remember the content of the last presentation you went to. If you happen to sit through a presentation, at the end of the presentation, try to write down everything you understood or took in.

This business statement will be the backbone of what you are selling. Don't worry: our map will show you the way.

Share Your Feelings

As we are talking about true things, I would like to spice things up just a little more.

We also have to be true to our feelings.

At the beginning of my career, I would become tense during meetings, especially when things didn't go as I had planned. One day I had scheduled a meeting with a contact, and at the meeting, I found that he had brought along a group of seven people. I froze up at that moment. I absolutely went blank, and the meeting was a total disaster.

How did I analyze the situation, and how did I resolve this problem?

I was not true to my feelings and my contacts. By trying to manage my feelings, I went blank during my presentation. So I resolved that during future meetings, I would be more honest about my feelings!

Okay, so what does that mean in practice?

Strategically speaking, in similar situations, tell your contacts things like this:

- Wow, I didn't expect so many people—now I am a fish out of water!
- I forgot what I was going to say. Give me just one second!
- If I had known, I would have called my backup team!

In other words, show your contacts your feelings. Not only will you win them over; you will no longer have to manage what you are feeling, and your presentation will then flow easily.

Please note that you should begin the meeting asking the participants about their expectations. This allows you to relax even more, and at the same time, your risk of error is smaller. You will be able to use the right words for the right people. You will say what they want to hear.

Final Word

I have a clear vision of what the future has in store for us in sales. I believe in three specific points:

1) **Psychology:** To deal with people, you need to read about this science. It will be the future of all relationships, personal and business. Is important to know how we really work.

2) **Processes:** It will be fundamental for the sales executive to understand project management. Clients' purchasing processes have become longer and more complex. Each sales opportunity will be a project.

3) **Execution**

   Here are three concepts:
   - **Strategy:** Where do I want to go?
   - **Tactics:** How do I get there? What is the best path?
   - **Techniques:** How do I want to get there?

Currently, most companies have strategy, and they know where they want to go; they also know how they want to get there. The sales executive's main contribution will be in regard to the company's tactics. Currently, this professional goes to several corporations and employs numerous tactics that companies use to reach their goals. And since tactics involve a practical, hands-on process, clients seek that attitude. Make it happen on the job.

Gaps refer to the empty spaces that are not filled. Sales executives that perceive and employ tactics to detect and help his clients with these gaps will have an essential tool for establishing a partnership.

A basis for these conclusions is the fact that everyday clients are more resistant to products and more predisposed to services. And this is our suggestion for how you, your team, and your company should work.

Now, for my last words, I will share with you the secret of the WinnersMap methodology.

Below, you have two maps. Map B is a demonstration of where I applied each psychological strength. Enjoy.

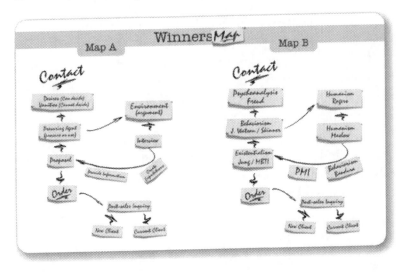

We've passed through a lot of thinking and internal questioning in this book. We started with concepts to get everybody on the same level. Then we passed through some important principles of sales and psychology. And in the end we summed up and delivered a map.

But the truth is that my personal goal was to get you exercising.

Yes! I wanted to get you exercising your mind. Use the art of thinking, and never stop exercising your mind. You will find that is a lot of fun, and it is good for the mind, body, and soul.

As we say here in Brazil, "filosofando"—to practice philosophy.

Thanks. It was a great journey, and I hope you enjoyed it.